P9-CAH-097

# African Crafts

# African Crafts

## Judith Hoffman Corwin

FRANKLIN WATTS

New York/London/Toronto/Sydney/1990

*Also by Judith Hoffman Corwin*

COLONIAL AMERICAN CRAFTS: THE HOME
COLONIAL AMERICAN CRAFTS: THE SCHOOL
COLONIAL AMERICAN CRAFTS: THE VILLAGE
PAPERCRAFTS

## For Jules Arthur and Oliver Jamie

Library of Congress Cataloging-in-Publication Data

Corwin, Judith Hoffman.
    African crafts / by Judith Hoffman Corwin.
      p.  cm.
    Includes index.
    Summary: Shows how to design masks, beads, toys, and other African
crafts using simple household materials.
    ISBN 0-531-10846-5
    1. Handicraft—Africa—Juvenile literature.  [1. Handicraft—
Africa.]  I. Title.
TT115.C65  1990
745.5—dc20                  90-12493 CIP AC

Copyright © 1990 by Judith Hoffman Corwin
All rights reserved
Printed in the United States of America
6 5 4 3

# Contents

# Introduction

Africa is the second-largest continent on earth, a land of mighty rivers, vast lakes, scorching deserts, snow-capped mountains, fertile plains, and dense rain forests. Africa's ancient history and culture are today being rediscovered with ever-greater interest, even as the landscape and daily lives of its people are being changed by the struggle for economic development.

In this book, you will learn how to make things in the style of both ancient and modern Africa, using materials that can be found in your home. The ancient African culture produced some of the most beautiful art and exciting objects ever made. These tribespeople made masks and dolls out of wood, sculptures out of clay, jewelry decorated with brightly colored beads, and cloths with pictures of wild animals on them.

Through art, young people can learn something about the history and customs of Africa. Art enriches both our understanding and respect for other peoples and cultures. Through projects inspired by African objects and foods, ordinary everyday materials can be messengers of this faraway continent.

The crafts of both ancient and modern Africa are important because they have produced useful, decorative, and expressive objects. Craft techniques were often passed on from father to son and mother to daughter so that they would remain alive. Today they are a true link to a cultural past and heritage. Sculpture was used to communicate ideas. Symbols and abstractions were not just used as beautiful decorations but were also useful and often had a religious or spiritual meaning. Handsome work was created without the use of sophisticated tools or expensive materials.

This book is filled with ideas, information, folklore, recipes, and games from the world of Africa. They help to show that crafts know no boundaries—they are a basic human expression. After all, there is only one world.

By following the clear and simple instructions included, you will be able to make many attractive things. Explore and appreciate how African artists create designs in their own special way to capture the unique spirit of their continent. You will also want to experiment and create your very own projects.

# Traditional African Designs

On the next few pages, you will see a fascinating, diverse selection of traditional African designs. There are simple, abstract, and geometric ones. There are designs of people and flowers. There are also animal designs to choose from—snake, frog, bird, zebra, elephant, lion, tiger, turtle, horse, goat, butterfly, lizard, hippopotamus, fish, rooster, leopard, antelope, and monkey. They can all be used on stationery, greeting cards, wrapping paper, pictures, and T-shirts. Just use your imagination. These wonderful designs can serve as inspiration for your own original drawings. You can have fun drawing them larger or smaller, and changing them as you like. To begin, all you need is a pencil and a piece of paper.

# African Beads

Beads are often worn in Africa and are an important part of Africa's cultural heritage. Their designs, patterns, and colors express positions in society, religion, politics, and style. Throughout the vast and diverse African continent—the deserts, tropical rain forests, woodlands, fertile river valleys, and grassy plains—the people all wear beads.

## HERE'S WHAT YOU WILL NEED:

2 cups flour, 1 cup salt, 1 cup water to make the "clay"
measuring cup, large bowl, toothpick, cookie sheet
red, yellow, orange, blue, green, white, brown, and black
   acrylic paints
shellac, brushes
24″ length of colored string or thread

## HERE'S HOW TO DO IT:

**1.** Read through all the directions for making the flour "clay" on page 35.

**2.** To make the beads, form small balls out of the dough. They should be about ½″ to 1″ high. Experiment with the different shapes as shown in the illustration. You will need about twenty beads for each necklace.

**3.** Push the toothpick through the center of each bead to make the hole to string it on.

**4.** For baking the beads, follow the directions given for the Baule and Ashanti gold weights on page 37.

**5.** Now you are ready to decorate your beads by painting them, following the designs given. Shellac the beads after you have decorated them and let them dry overnight.

**6.** String the beads on the thread and tie a double knot when they are the right length on you. About a 24″ length of string will make a nice necklace that will easily fit over your head. The beads don't have to go all the way around the thread.

# Mankala—An African Board Game

Throughout history, games have been a part of people's lives everywhere. For centuries, a board game of concentration and great fun has been played all over Africa. East Africans call the game Mankala; in the west it is called Oware or Ayo, and in the south Ohoro.

The Mankala playing board is sometimes elaborately carved and beautifully decorated. But the basic design of the board is so simple that some Africans just scoop twelve holes out of the sand and begin to play. Our board is also simple—it can be put together from an egg carton in a few minutes. The forty-eight playing pieces, or *hasa*, as they are called, can be any small, same-size objects. They can be rocks, shells, nuts, dried beans, seeds, buttons, beads, or even marbles.

## HERE'S WHAT YOU WILL NEED:

a clean egg carton, white or gray, with little or no printing on it (one made to hold 12 eggs)

15″ × 3″ piece of heavy cardboard, for the base

2 small paper cups, scissors, glue

48 objects for *hasa* (marbles, rocks, shells, nuts, dried beans, seeds, buttons, or beads); they should be ¼″ to ½″ around and all about the same size

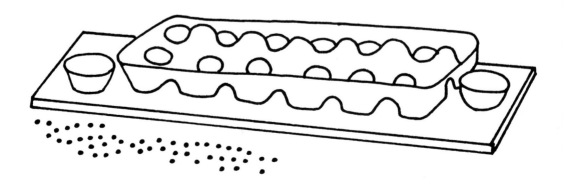

## HERE'S HOW TO DO IT:

**1.** Cut off the top of the egg carton. You are going to use just the bottom part.

**2.** Glue the bottom of the carton to the middle of the piece of cardboard. Cut the top off each of the paper cups so that only about 2″ of each cup remains. Glue each cup to the board, as shown in the illustration.

**3.** Put aside the forty-eight objects you have decided to use. Review the rules for the game, which follow, and then start to play. Good luck!

## RULES FOR PLAYING MANKALA

The game is played with two opponents facing each other across the board. Each player has six cups (compartments in the egg carton) on his side. Each cup contains four of the playing pieces (like seeds or marbles). An empty bank is on the end *to his right* (the paper cup). The game begins when the first player picks up the four pieces from *any cup on his side* and distributes them one by one, beginning with the cup immediately to the right of the empty one, and continuing counterclockwise around the board. He picks up all of the pieces from the cup into which he drops the last piece. He continues in this fashion, leaving the last cup empty and dropping his next piece into the next cup. His turn ends when he drops his last piece into an empty cup.

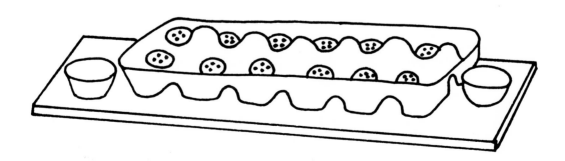

Points are always scored in groups of four pieces. Whenever the first player drops his *last* piece into a cup that already has three (giving the cup four pieces), he collects those four for his bank and his turn is over. If he drops a fourth piece (not his last) into a cup *during* a move, however, the four pieces immediately go to his opponent. The first player does not collect the four pieces unless the fourth piece was the *last* one in his hand. He finishes his turn by dropping his last piece into an empty cup or into a cup already containing three pieces.

During the player's turn, his opponent collects pieces for his bank every time the first player drops a fourth piece into a cup already containing three, unless the fourth piece was the first player's last piece.

When the first player's turn ends, his opponent takes up the pieces from *any cup on his side* and distributes them in the same way. The game continues until all of the pieces are collected in the banks. The player who collects the next-to-the-last four pieces earns the last four as a bonus. The player who has collected the most pieces wins the round, and takes over any one cup on his opponent's side as his own. The game can end at any time decided in advance by the players. It can end after a certain number of plays or after one player scores 100 points, or it can go on until one player has taken over all of his opponent's cups.

# Benin Leopard— A Royal Symbol

To the Benin people of Nigeria, the leopard is a symbol of the king—strong, fierce, and clever.

The Nigerian kings, or *obas*, lived in great walled palaces that had live leopards living inside. These royal leopards had been captured and tamed especially for the king.

Let's take this symbol on page 23 and draw it onto a *dashiki*, which is a West African shirt. Dashikis are very easy to make out of a rectangular piece of muslin or an old white sheet. In Africa they are made out of brightly colored and boldly patterned fabric with embroidered detailing. The leopard design can be drawn on with a black felt-tip marker. Try decorating your shirt with some of the designs on pages 8–15. You can even write your West African name—just look on page 42. Using the colored felt-tip markers, you can also decorate your dashiki.

## HERE'S WHAT YOU WILL NEED:

tape measure
2 yards of muslin or an old white sheet
pencil, scissors, glue, cardboard
black felt-tip marker and colored markers

## HERE'S HOW TO DO IT:

**1.** Check the illustration for the pattern, and you will see that the dashiki has only two seams and a neck opening. You will only have to cut the fabric in two places. This pattern is very easy to measure and make.

**2.** Have an adult help you with this part. Raise your arms out from the shoulders and have the other person measure you across from elbow to elbow. Now measure from your shoulder down to where your shirt usually ends. Double the measurement of the length from neck to waist. Cut a rectangle this size. Fold it in half, as shown, and cut an oval for the neckline, making sure that your head fits through. Cut out the side piece below the sleeves, as shown.

**3.** Open up the shirt, and with a pencil, lightly sketch in the Benin leopard design, as shown, and then anything else that you would like to decorate your shirt with.

**4.** Slip the cardboard inside the shirt to prevent the markers from going through the fabric. Go over the pencil lines with the black felt-tip marker and color in with the other markers. You can repeat steps 3 and 4 if you want to decorate both sides of your dashiki.

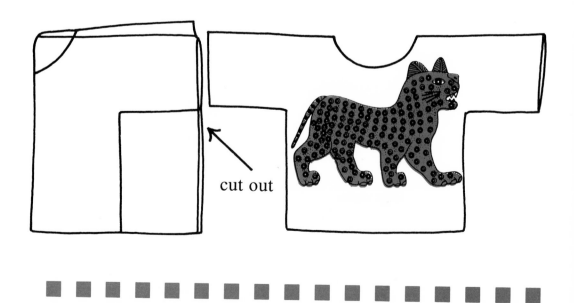

cut out

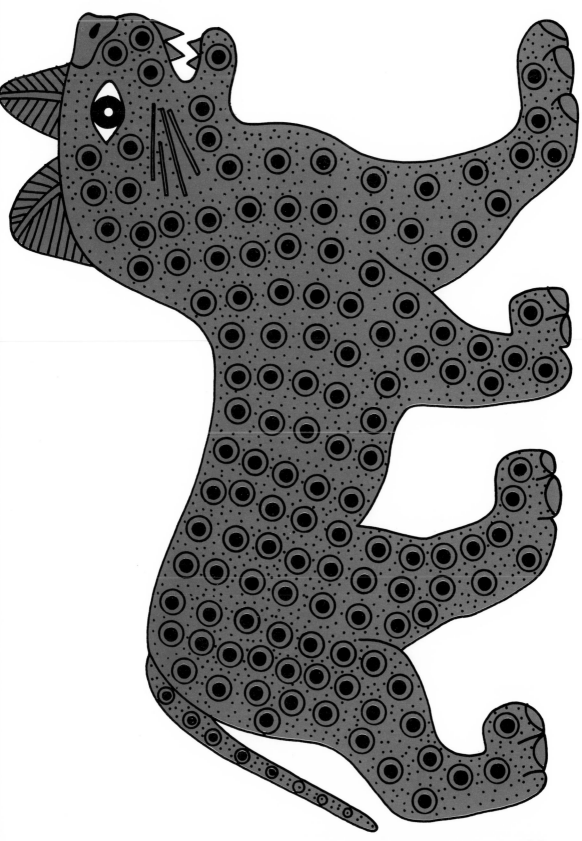

# "All the Birds Are Here"— Nigerian Cloth

These blue-and-white resist-dyed cloths are extremely decorative with their many bold designs and patterns. Some of the cloths also tell a story, like this one. The different combinations of designs give each cloth its name. The designs are drawn freehand onto the cloth with paint, and then the cloth is dipped into indigo (blue powder from plants) dye. Nigerians use special paint that resists the dye so the images stand out. We are going to be using crayons to draw on our cloth, and blue fabric dye to color it. Draw the center bird design onto your cloth, as shown in the illustration, and then experiment with the other patterns and designs that you can use from pages 8–15 to create your own special storytelling cloth.

## HERE'S WHAT YOU WILL NEED:

1 yard of muslin, 24" × 36"
yellow crayon (for best results), tape
1"-wide brush, blue liquid fabric dye, small bowl, newspaper

## HERE'S HOW TO DO IT:

**1.** Tape the four corners of your cloth onto the floor. This will keep it straight so that it will be easy to draw on.

**2.** Starting in the center of the cloth, draw the bird designs. You should draw them larger than they appear in the book, about 6" high. Have fun drawing the birds and other designs, and don't worry if they don't come out perfect. This cloth should look very expressive and should be done with big, bold strokes of the crayon. Checking the illustration, fill up the whole cloth with whatever designs and patterns you like.

**3.** Now spread out several layers of newspaper on the floor. Remove the tape from your cloth and put the cloth onto the newspaper. Tape each corner to the newspaper. Now you are ready to paint over your designs.

**4.** We are going to have to dilute the fabric dye, so an adult should help you with this. Put one capful of the dye into the small bowl. Fill the bowl with water and stir the solution with the brush. With the brush, paint over your whole cloth. Where you have drawn with crayon on the cloth, the dye will resist and the drawing will show through. Carefully paint to the edges of the cloth, covering it entirely. Lift the tape after you have painted over everything else and put some paint where the tape was. Allow the cloth to dry. Now you can display your very own Nigerian cloth on the wall and admire your story.

# Creepy, Crawly Creatures

The spider, lizard, crocodile, and snake are all native to the African continent. Their designs will make creepy and crawly bookmarks that have small, plain white buttons on them. African craftsmen used these same buttons on many of their things to help decorate them.

■ ■ ■ ■ ■ ■ ■ ■ ■ ■ ■ ■ ■ ■ ■ ■ ■ ■

## HERE'S WHAT YOU WILL NEED:

1 sheet of white oaktag
tracing paper, carbon paper, pencil, scissors, pin, string
25 small white buttons, white glue
black fine-line felt-tip marker
green and brown felt-tip markers

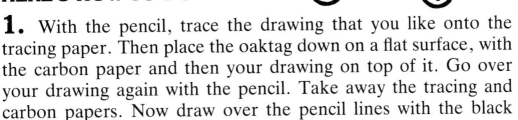

## HERE'S HOW TO DO IT:

**1.** With the pencil, trace the drawing that you like onto the tracing paper. Then place the oaktag down on a flat surface, with the carbon paper and then your drawing on top of it. Go over your drawing again with the pencil. Take away the tracing and carbon papers. Now draw over the pencil lines with the black fine-line felt-tip marker. Cut out the drawing. This step is the same for the spider, lizard, crocodile, and snake.

**2.** Glue buttons onto the spider for his eyes, as shown. The spider can also be hung up. Make a small hole with the pin at the top of his head. Put some string through the hole, and your spider is ready to hang up.

**3.** The lizard should be colored in with the brown felt-tip marker and his eyes glued on.

**4.** Color in the crocodile with the green felt-tip marker. The crocodile's bumps on his back are made from buttons. Glue them on, as shown.

**5.** The snake should also be colored in green felt-tip marker and buttons should be glued to his skin, as shown.

# Ivory Coast Baule Mask

The mask plays a very important part in African tribal ceremonies. Many of the masks are worn by members of secret groups that run the tribe. They train the young people in the ways of the tribe. These members wear masks and costumes so that they can speak to the spirits and keep evil forces away. The tribespeople believe that a man disguised in a mask and costume can be changed into a spirit himself. The spirit—a powerful, mysterious being—will speak through the man.

Most of the African masks were carved out of wood and then decorated in various ways. This mask is going to be made out of papier-mâché and painted. There are two different designs for the mask. Choose whichever one you want to make.

## HERE'S WHAT YOU WILL NEED:

1 large sheet of newspaper, 28″ × 22″
basic paste (see page 32)
transparent tape, scissors
4 pieces of 8½″ × 11″ white paper
black and white poster paint, paintbrush, scrap of cardboard
10 large sheets of newspaper, torn into strips 6″ × 1″
2″ piece of heavy string

## HERE'S HOW TO DO IT:

**1.** Tightly crumple up the large sheet of newspaper and shape it into a ball. Use a few pieces of tape to help it stay together.

**2.** Crumple up each sheet of white paper and shape into horns and ears. Dip them into the paste, squeezing out the extra, and attach to the mask, as shown in the illustration.

**3.** Cut the eyes and mouth out of the cardboard, as shown in the illustration. With extra paste, attach to the mask.

**4.** Dip the strips of newspaper into the paste and squeeze out the extra paste with your fingers. Cover the entire oval with three layers of newspaper strips.

**5.** Allow it to dry overnight.

**6.** Cover the mask with the black paint; allow it to dry. Decorate it with the white paint, as shown in the illustration.

**7.** Fold the string in half and tape it to the top edge of the mask. Now your Baule mask is ready to hang.

## PASTE RECIPE

### HERE'S WHAT YOU WILL NEED:

measuring cup and spoon
1 cup white flour
1 tablespoon salt
1 cup water
large mixing bowl
mixing spoon

### HERE'S HOW TO DO IT:

**1.** Combine the flour and salt in the large mixing bowl. Gradually add the water. Stir the mixture for several minutes. It will be lumpy and look like thick cream.

**2.** Store any leftover paste in a covered jar in the refrigerator. It will keep for about a week.

33

# Baule and Ashanti Gold Weights

These animal-shaped gold weights were used three hundred years ago in the Ivory Coast and Ghana. Baule and Ashanti men carried their own scale, gold dust, and these weights with them when they were trading. A weight on one side of the scale balanced the proper amount of gold dust on the other. These weights came in graduated sizes and various shapes. Designs are given here for a frog, porcupine, snake, chameleon, duck, antelope, elephant, and fish. They will be made out of a flour and salt "clay."

## HERE'S WHAT YOU WILL NEED:

measuring cup
2 cups flour, 1 cup salt, 1 cup water, to make the "clay"
large bowl
tracing paper
cardboard
pencil, scissors
knife, rolling pin, potholder
strainer
toothpick
cookie sheet
yellow or gold acrylic paints
shellac, brushes
colored string or ribbon

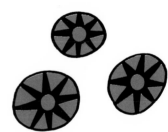

## HERE'S HOW TO DO IT:

**1.** Mix the flour and salt together in a large bowl. Then add the water a little at a time, mixing it in. When all the water is used up, mix the dough well with your hands. This is called "kneading."

**2.** Continue to knead the dough until it is smooth.

**3.** Put some flour on a clean working surface and then roll the dough to about ¼" thickness. (The dough will expand slightly when it is baked.)

**4.** Trace the pattern of the weight you want from the book onto the tracing paper and then transfer it to the cardboard, and cut it out.

**5.** Place the cardboard cutout on the dough. Hold the cardboard down with one hand, and use your knife carefully to cut the dough around the pattern.

**6.** Roll small pieces of dough for eyes, cheeks, and other features. Put some dough through a sieve (strainer) to make hair. Moisten the weight with a drop of water; then put on the dough decorations. Moistening makes them stick better.

**7.** With a toothpick, make a hole at the top of the weight so you can hang it up if you like. Or you can wear one around your neck.

**8.** *An adult should help you with this step and step 9.* Set the oven at 325°F. Place the weights on a cookie sheet at least 1″ apart and bake until lightly browned. It takes about 15 to 20 minutes, but keep checking the oven to make sure that the ornaments aren't burning along the edges.

**9.** Using a potholder to protect your hand, remove the cookie sheet from the oven. When the weights are cool, take them off the cookie sheet.

**10.** Color your weights with the acrylic paint.

**11.** When the weights are dry, cover them completely with shellac to keep out any moisture and to preserve them.

**12.** You can put some string through the holes in the weights. This way you can hang them up or wear one as a necklace. They are also fun just as they are.

# Grigri—An African "Good Luck" Charm

Years ago, grigris were worn all over Africa. They were thought to ward off evil and to help the wearers control the supernatural forces around them. They were made of many different materials—leather, fibers, bone, ivory, metal, and even gold. Each material and decorative symbol had a particular magical quality. Today they are mostly worn in North Africa, where they are made from leather with printed protective designs and symbols on them.

## HERE'S WHAT YOU WILL NEED:

heavy cardboard (3″ square)
24″ piece of string to hang your pendant on
black felt-tip marker and colored markers
scissors

## HERE'S HOW TO DO IT:

**1.** Choose which of the grigri designs you would like to make.

**2.** Cut your cardboard out; check the illustration.

**3.** With the black felt-tip marker, draw the design onto your cardboard. Color in with the other markers.

**4.** Make a hole, as shown, on your grigri, and put the string through it. Adjust the string to the length that you want and then tie the ends together. Cut off any excess string.

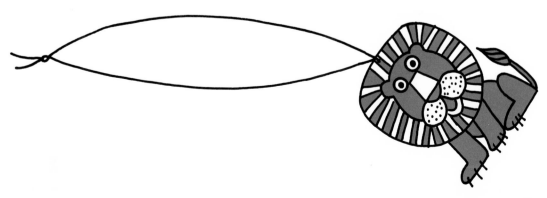

# Ashanti Doll

Women of the Ashanti tribe, who live in Ghana, who are going to have a baby carry this decorative doll tucked into the waistband of their dresses. They believe that this *akua-ba*, as it is called, will bring them a healthy and beautiful child.

## HERE'S WHAT YOU WILL NEED:

tracing paper, carbon paper, tape
8½″ × 11″ piece of heavy cardboard
glue, pencil, scissors
black fine-line felt-tip marker
small colorful beads (about 30), needle, thread

## HERE'S HOW TO DO IT:

**1.** Place a sheet of tracing paper over the design for the doll and trace the doll.

**2.** Place a sheet of carbon paper over the cardboard that you will be using to make the doll. On top of the carbon paper, place the tracing paper with the design on it.

**3.** Tape the three sheets together at the top and bottom of your work surface. This will prevent the papers from sliding around as you draw. Draw over the design on the tracing paper.

**4.** Remove the tracing and carbon papers. With the black fine-line felt-tip marker, draw over the design. Cut it out.

**5.** On the pattern there are two small dots where the doll's earrings should go. Thread the needle and then string some beads onto it. Use about eight to ten beads for each earring. With the needle, put a hole where a dot is and then insert the thread through it. Tie the ends together to attach the earring to the doll. Repeat on the other side. Make a necklace for the doll and tie it around her neck. Check the illustration to see how these ornaments are attached and how the necklace should look.

# West African Names—Stationery

The Akan tribe of West Africa believes that a person's first name is his soul name. It is taken from the name of the day that he or she is born on.

The Akan believe there are seven different kinds of life-souls—one for each day of the week—and people born on the same day have the same kind of soul. Ask your parents what day of the week you were born on so that you can find out your Akan name. Write it on a piece of paper and then draw some African designs around it to make an interesting picture. Look at pages 8–15 for some design ideas.

## HERE'S WHAT YOU WILL NEED:

8½″ × 11″ sheet of white paper
red fine-line felt-tip marker
black fine-line felt-tip marker

## HERE'S HOW TO DO IT:

**1.** Find your Akan name and write it on the center of the paper. Use the red fine-line felt-tip marker to do this.

**2.** Look at pages 8–15 for some designs that you would like to draw around your name. You can choose animals or simple geometric patterns. Check the illustration for ideas.

**3.** Use the black fine-line felt-tip marker to make your designs.

| DAY OF THE WEEK | | GIRL'S NAME | BOY'S NAME |
|---|---|---|---|
| Monday | (Dwoda) | Adwoa | Kwadwo |
| Tuesday | (Benada) | Abena | Kwabena |
| Wednesday | (Wukuda) | Akua | Kwaku |
| Thursday | (Yawda) | Yaa | Yaw |
| Friday | (Fida) | Afua | Kofi |
| Saturday | (Memeneda) | Ama | Kwame |
| Sunday | (Kwasida) | Akosua | Kwasi |

# Couscous—An Algerian Chicken Stew

Chicken is served on special occasions in Africa, and couscous is a delicious chicken stew that is cooked in one large pot.

## HERE'S WHAT YOU WILL NEED:

### Ingredients

1 chicken, cut into pieces
¼ cup olive oil
2 tablespoons butter
1 onion, cut into small pieces
1 large ripe tomato
1 teaspoon ground pepper
1 tablespoon ground cinnamon
1 teaspoon salt
1½ cups water
1 can chickpeas, with liquid
couscous-semolina grain (Couscous is a precooked grain that is available in packages in natural-food stores and in some supermarkets. Follow cooking instructions on the 8-ounce package.)

### Utensils

measuring cups and spoons
knife, large spoon to stir the stew
large covered pot
large serving bowl or platter

## HERE'S HOW TO DO IT:

**1.** Combine the chicken, oil, butter, onion, tomato, pepper, cinnamon, and salt in a large pot. *Ask an adult to help you now with the cooking.* Stir the mixture over medium heat until the chicken is brown. Turn chicken over and then brown that side.

**2.** Add water and bring to a boil. Simmer, covered, for about an hour, until the chicken is tender. Be sure to check while the chicken is cooking to see if you need to add more water. If more is needed, add about a cup.

**3.** Add the chickpeas and their liquid. Continue to cook the stew for another half hour.

**4.** To serve the stew in a traditional manner, put the cooked couscous on the serving platter and then spoon on as much liquid from the stew as the couscous will absorb. Pile the chicken in the center. Serves four to six.

# Injera–Ethiopian Flat Bread

These are flat and airy round breads that are perfect to serve with the couscous. They have a slightly spongy texture.

## HERE'S WHAT YOU WILL NEED:

### Ingredients

4 cups self-rising flour
1 cup whole wheat flour
1 teaspoon baking powder
2 cups club soda
water
vegetable oil to grease the
    frying pan

### Utensils

measuring cups and spoons
large mixing bowl and spoon
spatula, clean cloth
large platter
10″ nonstick frying pan

## HERE'S HOW TO DO IT:

**1.** Combine flours and baking powder in a bowl. Add club soda plus about 4 cups water. Mix into a smooth, fairly thin batter.

**2.** *Ask an adult to help you now with the frying.* Heat the nonstick frying pan. When a drop of water bounces on the pan's surface, dip enough batter from the bowl to cover the bottom of the pan. Pour it in quickly, all at once. Swirl the pan so that the entire bottom is evenly coated, then set it back on the heat.

**3.** When the moisture has evaporated and small holes appear on the surface of the batter, remove the injera. It should be cooked on only one side and not browned. If your first try is too pasty and undercooked, you may need to cook it a little longer or to make the next one thinner. Be careful not to cook it too long; it should be soft enough to fold.

**4.** Stack the injera one on top of the other as you cook, covering them with a clean cloth to prevent their drying out. To serve, lay them on a platter overlapping. Serves six to eight.

# Banana Fritters

Fried fruits and vegetables are quite popular all over the African continent. This makes a lovely dessert or a nice snack.

## HERE'S WHAT YOU WILL NEED:

### Ingredients

1¼ cups flour
¼ cup sugar
1 teaspoon ground cinnamon
1 egg
½ cup milk
3 medium-size bananas, mashed
oil for deep-frying
confectioners' sugar

### Utensils

measuring cups and spoons
large mixing bowl and spoon
sturdy wire whisk
frying pan and spatula
slotted spoon
paper towels
serving platter

## HERE'S HOW TO DO IT:

**1.** In a large mixing bowl, combine flour, sugar, and cinnamon. Beat in the egg, using the wire whisk. Gradually add the milk, continuing to beat until batter is smooth and satiny, about 5 minutes. Stir in the bananas and let the mixture sit while the oil is heating.

**2.** *Ask an adult to help you now with the frying.* Use a medium-high flame on the stove to heat the oil. Take out about ¼ cup of the batter and pour it, all at once, quickly, into the hot oil. Let brown 2 to 3 minutes; then turn with the slotted spoon.

**3.** Be sure to watch carefully and remove fritters when they are a rich golden brown. Lay them on clean, absorbent paper towels to drain.

**4.** Continue frying until all the batter is used. Fry four or five fritters at a time. (If you want to save some of the batter for later use, cover the bowl tightly and refrigerate. The batter will turn a streaky brown, but will be good for two or three days.) Keep the first-cooked fritters warm in a low oven while you fry more, but eat them as soon as possible. Sprinkle with confectioners' sugar just before serving. Makes about ten fritters.

# Index